THE BOOK OF HOPE

Proven Secrets to Achieve Your Dreams and Live a Happier Life

Alex Dorcius

THE BOOK OF HOPE: Proven Secrets to Achieve Your Dreams and Live a Happier Life
www.BelieveYourHope.com
Copyright © 2023 Alex Dorcius

Paperback ISBN: 979-8-861439-74-9

All rights reserved. No portion of this book may be reproduced mechanically, electronically, or by any other means, including photocopying, without permission of the publisher or author except in the case of brief quotations embodied in critical articles and reviews. It is illegal to copy this book, post it to a website, or distribute it by any other means without permission from the publisher or author.

References to internet websites (URLs) were accurate at the time of writing. Authors and the publishers are not responsible for URLs that may have expired or changed since the manuscript was prepared.

Limits of Liability and Disclaimer of Warranty
The author and publisher shall not be liable for your misuse of the enclosed material. This book is strictly for informational and educational purposes only.

Warning – Disclaimer
The purpose of this book is to educate and entertain. The author and/or publisher do not guarantee that anyone following these techniques, suggestions, tips, ideas, or strategies will become successful. The author and/or publisher shall have neither liability nor responsibility to anyone with respect to any loss or damage caused, or alleged to be caused, directly or indirectly by the information contained in this book.

Medical Disclaimer
The medical or health information in this book is provided as an information resource only and is not to be used or relied on for any diagnostic or treatment purposes. This information is not intended to be patient education, does not create any patient-physician relationship, and should not be used as a substitute for professional diagnosis and treatment.

Publisher
10-10-10 Publishing
Markham, ON Canada

Printed in Canada and the United States of America

*To everyone who is in search of Hope.
To the one, who really wants to see the light
through the darkest side of life. And, more specially,
to all those who want to live a happier life.*

TABLE OF CONTENTS

Testimonial vii
Acknowledgments ix
Foreword xi
Introduction xiii

Chapter 1: There Is Always Hope 1
Chapter 2: Believe in Your Power and Authority 11
Chapter 3: Your Intention Is Powerful 21
Chapter 4: If You Know What You Want, You Can Get It 31
Chapter 5: Set Your Goals 45
Chapter 6: Imagination Will Lead You to Your Destination 53
Chapter 7: The Power of Your Words 65
Chapter 8: Gratitude 77
Chapter 9: Discipline, the Ugly Duckling of Success 87
Chapter 10: Hope, Prayer, and Faith 99

Conclusion 113
About the Author 117

Testimonial

My good friend Alex Dorcius doesn't just write these words; he lives by them every day. I have never seen Alex with anything but a smile on his face in the 3+ years I have known him. He is a special person who brings Hope, Peace, and Life to any occasion and knows how to make others lighten up and subconsciously impact their day positively. Alex's manual for positive living isn't just a psychological handbook or a spiritual betterment guide; but a practical application of a well-spent life. Congratulations to my good friend and brother on his accomplishment, and may God bless this work he has given us.

Co-worker
Michael Erdman

Acknowledgments

First, I'm grateful for God, who gives me hope and allows me to share that hope with anybody in need and the world in general.

I'm also grateful for the following special people...

My mother, Anne Antoinette Dorcius, a woman I love so much. I'm told that after I was delivered, the placenta remained in her womb for about eight hours. There was no emergency system or 911 to call because it was a home delivery in the countryside. She could have died for me. Thank you, Mom!

My dad, Joseph E. Dorcius. He was a man of great dreams and courage who worked hard to care for his family and neighbors. Before passing, he told me, "Alex, my son, life is short. If you have to do something, do it now." I will never forget that.

My wife, Margalie Dorcius, who inspired me to write this book.

And I thank all my brothers and sisters—Jean Renold, Pierre Rony, Marie Veronique, Marie Edwidge, Max E., Phanuel, Altagrace, Cerette, Dorothie, and Francis. They love me unconditionally and trust my leadership in everything I do.

Certainly, this project wouldn't be possible without the help of some terrific people in my extended community, whether directly or indirectly.

For bonuses go to www.BelieveYourHope.com

Therefore, I wish to express my thanks to...

- Father Reginald Jean-Mary, administrator of Notre Dame D'Haiti Church in Miami, Florida
- Mike Erdman and Freddie Erdman, owners of Erdman Automotive
- My friends Yanm Morales, Michael Erdman, Joel Jerome, Adelson Pierre, and others
- Multiple award-winning author Clayton Bye
- *New York Times* bestselling author Raymond Aaron
- Marie E. Dorcius Pierre, author of the book *Creating Your Own Success*
- The late Alcimond Colas, one of the most outstanding leaders I've ever known
- Les Brown, one of the most incredible public speakers in the world
- Stephen Golberg, the late Dexter Yager, PJ Smith, and Mitch Bernnott

There are many other people to be grateful for, so I thank everyone who gave me advice.

God bless you all.

Foreword

Alex Dorcius is a rare example of the power of attitude. I've never seen him without a smile, and the man exudes such energy that you cannot help but notice his effect on the people around him. Alex has been through some harsh experiences, as you will discover when you read *The Book of Hope*. But instead of being soured on life, he found that hope can get you through the darkest days and has the power to lift and bring you back into the light.

I am not talking about the power of positive thinking. Alex's optimism, enthusiasm, and obvious peacefulness of spirit originate in something far more complex. He believes that you have the power and authority to command your destiny, and that maintaining hope for a better you and happier life is the secret to long-term motivation. It can keep you taking actions necessary for success even when all indicators point to failure. And I must stress how important that is. Don't quit before achieving the success you desire; all you need to do is keep pushing forward.

Alex also identifies many tools you can use to build on the foundation of hope he wants to help you find. This book, which might initially seem to be spiritual, is a practical treasure trove designed to help you achieve the life of your dreams. So I encourage you to study the words of this remarkable man and take his advice to heart. It might just revolutionize your life!

Raymond Aaron
***New York Times* Bestselling Author**

Introduction

Hope is an optimistic state of mind based on your expectation of positive outcomes concerning events and circumstances; it's the good things you desire in the future.

Every human being is born with hope, and we relate to it before all else. However, some people lose hope through fear, failure, or sticking themselves under a self-made ceiling, thinking it's over and there's no more reason to exist. But hope is infinite, and wherever there's hope, there's life. Furthermore, hope is available for everyone, regardless of race, religion, or sex. Even *The Bible* says there's surely a future hope for you—one that won't be cut off. However, while "hope springs eternal," it's up to you to find the hope that applies to you.

The Bible also says, "So we fix our eyes not on what is seen, but on what is unseen, since what is seen is temporary, but what is unseen is eternal." Consequently, when you finally achieve whatever you were hoping for, it's imperative to celebrate your success. You also need to understand that since your achievement is now "seen," you can no longer consider it as "hope." And this is where you need to be careful because reaching the level of success where you think you've arrived at the top is dangerous, and it's where countless people fail.

For bonuses go to ...

I've seen many famous people, successful businessmen and women, TV moguls, and superstars you might think have arrived at their destination of abundance, but many still destroy themselves. Among them, I'm reminded of the great American actor Robin Williams, who brought joy to everyone but couldn't see it for himself, and the late Stephen Boss, a famous DJ for the Ellen Degeneres show, who committed suicide. The rich and famous get hopeless, just as the middle class and poor get hopeless. So wouldn't you agree that hope is more significant than money, success, and fame?

In the following chapters, I'll talk about cultivating hope, seeing it for yourself—even if you may be in the darkest moment of your life—and maintaining it to attain your dreams. But first, my story...

In 2010, I was doing well as a new car salesman at a Toyota dealership based in Miami, Florida. I could pay my bills but wanted to make more money and create a better lifestyle. I had big dreams. One day a co-worker came to me with an idea about a network marketing company that could make us a lot of money. Following my dreams, I decided to keep working in the dealership but would join the network marketing organization as a side hustle. The company was Gano Excel, and the products were exceptional—so good that my business moved fast, and I qualified to go to a seminar in California. I went to the dealership's General Sales Manager and asked him for a few days off. He said okay, but I didn't get it in writing, and I was so excited that I left without asking him for confirmation. Little did I know that someone reported I was at a business seminar. Consequently, when I returned, he fired me for leaving without permission. I didn't quit; he fired me.

I threw myself one hundred percent into the business, traveling from city to city and state to state, giving presentations everywhere in the United States. My business expanded, and I even traveled to Canada a couple of times. First, I went to Montreal, where I had a group multiplying daily, and then to Ottawa. I was like a superstar and extremely happy with my lifestyle.

However, sometimes bad things happen to good people. Gano Excel was based in Asia, with a branch in California. One day, the US CEO and his management team decided to create their own products and sever ties with Malaysia. But the new company couldn't duplicate the Gano Excel products; they just weren't as good. Consequently, we lost our credibility, and most affiliates left the company. As you might guess, my income crashed to the floor. It wasn't long before we began moving from apartment to apartment because we couldn't pay our rent.

At the beginning of 2013, my wife and I lived on the first floor of an apartment building in Miami Gardens, Florida. The apartment was extremely humid, and the bathroom backed up now and then. I remember one of my sisters-in-law coming to visit, and instead of enjoying her stay, she became a bathroom cleaner because every time there was a backup, we had to clean quickly to avoid insect invasion. It was unhealthy, to say the least.

The misery just added to an already untenable situation. We were barely surviving and couldn't pay our rent. The landlord allowed us to stay for the month of February if we promised to pay. However, on February 28th, when we still didn't have the

For bonuses go to ...

money, he kicked us out, and we became homeless. We slept in a Toyota Tundra pickup belonging to one of my good friends, "mi hermano" Yanm Morales. I will always be grateful to God and him.

I remember picking my wife up from church late one evening. Like everybody else, we took the 95 expressway and drove north. I looked at her, and she looked at me, and she said, "Everybody is going somewhere, and we don't even know where we're going." We laughed and laughed and laughed. Such moments were rare, though, and life was hard.

That night, we slept in the Jackson North Hospital parking lot, and it was so cold that my wife cried like a baby. I couldn't afford to put the truck heater on because we were short on gas. The truck was cramped, and you couldn't stretch your legs. We went to sleep late and woke up early every day so we could go to public restrooms to clean up. A proper shower wasn't an option, but we did manage to go to the beach once a week. It wasn't easy because we had to pay $5 to enter with the truck. Imagine it! One bath a week during a hot Miami summer.

One day, after soaking ourselves at the beach, I remember we went in the sweet water to rinse off. While we were in the shower, our faces and bodies covered with soap, two old ladies who wanted to rinse themselves got mad at us. My wife and I talked and said, "Those two ladies don't understand that they come to rinse, but we are here to take our only shower for the week."

I remember it being so hot one night at the beginning of July 2013 that I woke up early and went to wash up in a McDonald's restaurant in Miami. After locking the door, I took off all my clothes, got my towel and a piece of soap, and started my special bath. The door flew open, and a man walked in.

I said, "Haaaaaaaa!"

And the guy said, "Haaaaaa! I'm sorry."

Then he closed the door and left.

Later that day, I told my wife the story, and we laughed as we had never laughed before.

Then there was the time the pickup truck that was our home and only means of transportation ran out of gas. We turned the truck upside down, searching everywhere, and finally came up with 75 cents. When we got to the gas station, I didn't want people to hear how much fuel I was buying, so I gave the cashier the 75 cents and said, "Pump two."

Ladies and gentlemen, we drove that V8 Tundra for a week on just 75 cents worth of gas. It was a miracle, and I believe that God was with us. Thus, I became more and more positive and hopeful that we would get out of the misery.

What happened after that miraculous week, however, is that we ran out of everything. My wife and I didn't have so much as a penny, so I raised my eyes to the sky and prayed, "Dear God, I believe you're here with me. I come to you this morning because I really need you, and I need you now."

After a while, I found myself repeating Psalm 34, verse 4: "I sought the Lord, and he answered me; He delivered me from all my fears." It left me feeling utterly at peace. And as the day progressed and I thought about what to do next, I realized there was still one asset I could use. It was nothing less than my wedding ring. So I went to a jewelry store and sold it.

That money kept us for quite a while. Of course, my wife

For bonuses go to ...

eventually asked me about the missing wedding ring.

"We ate it," I said.

"What do you mean we ate it?"

There was nothing to do but tell her the truth.

"I sold it so that we could eat."

I could see the tears forming in her eyes, so I gave her a big hug and a kiss and said, "You know what? The most important thing is that we're still married."

On August 28th, 2013, six months after becoming homeless, we were finally able to rent a one-bedroom apartment—a veritable mansion to us. Moreover, two years later, I went to my banker for approval to buy a house, and after checking my credit and income, he told me, "My friend, you're the most powerful man walking in the street."

I asked him, "Why?"

He answered, "Not only have you qualified to buy a home, but you can buy a million-dollar house right now if you want."

That was mind-blowing to me. To learn I was qualified to buy a million-dollar house just two years after being homeless was a true "WOW moment." But it was just one stop on a fantastic journey. Since then, I've reached almost every single goal I've set. I needed a bachelor's degree in Communication Arts and got it. Then, I wanted to be an author and wrote a book. I owe no student loan, travel wherever I want, live in a gorgeous house in the Sunshine State of Florida with a big yard and beautiful landscaping, and drive the car of my dreams.

Now that we're living a much better lifestyle, my wife has told me that in our most challenging moment in the street, she thought briefly about killing herself. But she also said I kept her from acting on that malicious idea because of how I handled the crisis, and the many uplifting things I repeatedly did or said. When I heard this, I felt goosebumps all over my body, and I asked myself, "Why not share this with the world?" Indeed, it's my understanding that millions of people are suffering worldwide because of financial issues, family problems, or depression and suicidal thoughts, and they don't know what to do; they are without hope. So, sharing my experience may help a few find something they can do to accomplish their dreams and live a happier, better life.

How did I handle the crisis? What are those things I repeatedly do or say which turned my wife away from suicide and kept her hope alive? How did we survive the challenging moments? And how did I reach a place where I could have almost anything I wanted? In the following chapters, I propose to answer all these questions, so keep reading.

Chapter 1

There Is Always Hope

1

When you really know who you are, your thought process will change, and your life will ultimately morph. Hoping for a better you and a fulfilling existence plays a crucial role in that journey.

I want you to imagine you're an athlete participating in a marathon with about 100 million other athletes, and only one person can enter the final door. Then imagine all the other athletes becoming weak and falling on the road. You're the only one with the strength and power to reach the finish line and enter through that door. How would you feel? What would you think and say? In what manner would you celebrate?

My dear reader, I want to let you know that this isn't an imaginary exercise. It has already happened. You actually experienced such a thing, and it's why you're able to read my book today. You're a victor, champion, success, gift, and blessing. If that's not reason enough to hope for a bright future, I don't know what is.

For bonuses go to ...

Understand Who You Are

To better understand what I'm getting at, I propose illustrating scientifically and biblically where your power and authority originated, and how to reclaim them...

Science has demonstrated that it takes up to 100 million sperm to make a baby (based on a study from Harvard Center for Risk Analysis, in November 1997, entitled *Risk in Perspective*). Whether you raced against 5 million, 20 million, or 100 million sperm, you were the only one to reach the finish line and enter the door to life.

In *The Bible*, Genesis 1 says God created the heavens, earth, and universe. Then, God said, "Let us make mankind in our image, in our likeness, so that they may rule over the fish in the sea and the birds in the sky, over the livestock and all wild animals, and over all creatures that move along the ground." So God created human beings with full power; He gave us complete authority and kingship power. Elsewhere in *The Bible*, we read that God commanded that we "Be fruitful and increase in number, fill the earth and subdue it. Rule over the fish in the sea and the birds in the sky and over every living creature that moves on the ground." What a blessing!

That begs the question: If you were created in the likeness of God, given authority to rule, and blessed to be powerful, who can stop you? Winston Churchill once said, "When there is no enemy within, the enemies outside cannot hurt you." So, be your own friend, know yourself, and accept your power. Conversely, don't be your own enemy. Don't stop yourself. Let's go!

www.BelieveYourHope.com

A Light in the Darkness

I'm convinced you have all the power and authority to believe in whatever you want. My interest in writing this book isn't to push anyone to believe the things I do. Instead, I intend to project light into the darkness so that whoever wants to can see. I understand that we must learn daily—if we're to improve ourselves and our lives. The fact that you're reading this book proves you're a learner and looking for something. Well, guess what? What you're looking for is looking for you! *The Bible* said, "Seek, and you shall find." So, keep on seeking, and you'll keep on finding.

In that vein, I want to assure you that you were never alone, you aren't alone now, and you'll never be alone. You have within you the breath of God. You were made to His image and resemblance. So I believe it's safe to say God is always with you.

The problem I see is that most of the time, we're too busy in the world we live in to go within ourselves to talk to Him. Let today be a wake-up call that He is waiting to help and guide you. *The Bible* said in 1 John 4:4, "Ye are of God, little children, and have overcome; because greater is he that is in you, than he that is in the world." Today is the day to regain your God-given power and authority because the kingdom of God is within you.

Get Your Hopes Up!

It's about time to get your hopes up because when God, the creator of the universe, is with you, nothing can be against you, and everything is within reach. When I say everything is within your reach, I mean health, riches, joy, abundance, and so on. Thus, it's essential to know that you're a powerful human, and no one is better than you. If someone can do something, you can do it too, so achieving what you want is just a question of choice and qualification. Being in a lower position doesn't mean you're inferior to someone in a higher position, nor does it take away your God-given power and authority.

God created us to live together; we need each other to be complete. Consider the structure of a business organization: There are many positions—owner, CEO, CFO, directors, managers, assistant managers, associates, and housekeepers. If I asked which of these is more important, what would be your answer? You might say the owner or the CEO; however, I believe each occupies a different function, and no particular one is more important than another. Why? Because no owner or proprietor wants to have a filthy place, they need someone to clean, and no one in the business can do everything without the help of someone else. We all live in this world together and are bundled to use our power to help each other.

You Were Born to Rule

You're a powerful ruler. You have dominion power without border; should there be a border, you're the self-imposer. Nobody forces you to live where you're living, work where you're working, have what you're having, drive what you're driving, or keep or change the lifestyle that you're living. You choose those things and those situations. You're the ruler; you rule over yourself, your house, and your family.

Let me say this to you differently: you choose what you do and what you don't do. The problem is that most people choose to rule only occasionally, and let their cultures and environment rule over them the rest of the time. But make no mistake! You're a ruler, and your only limits are those you create. The truth is that you can have whatever you want, go wherever you wish, and have a lifestyle of your choice—if you decide to rule over these things.

Remember that among millions of sperm, you were the one, and only one, that was victorious. You forced your way into life, and your mom and dad welcomed you as a prince or a princess in this world. Now that you're an adult, it's time to become aware of your ruling power. You can rule to change your life and have the things you so passionately desire. You're a go-getter, champion, blessing, blesser, and co-creator; you're limitless. So go, raise your hopes, and design the lifestyle you want.

Regardless of whether or not you accept my words, I want to let you know that you're not just a simple human being; you're a powerful creature without limits. You're not just a little man or woman; you're a man or a woman equal to all others. Don't let colors or sizes fool you. It doesn't matter if you're white, black, yellow, red, short, or tall; we all have the same power. The spirit of God is always with us, so we only need to be aware and ask him for help when we're in need.

The Bible tells of a king and his entire country who feared a mighty warrior giant named Goliath, who had terrorized the king and his army for many days. Then came a short teenager named

For bonuses go to ...

David. When he discovered what was happening, David went straight to the king and accepted the challenge to kill Goliath with no sword or armor. Even David's brother belittled the young man. But David didn't listen because he knew that God was with him. He wasn't alone. With that in mind, the teenager killed Goliath with just a stone. David knew that he could do it, and he did.

The spirit of winning and strength and power David used to destroy Goliath was also with you when you were just one of a million sperm. That spirit guided you to victory, and I'm convinced it's still with you today. But you are the one who must decide to use it; nobody can do this for you. There's a sleeping giant within that can help you get everything you want in life. So, are you ready to wake the spirit, or will you let it sleep?

www.BelieveYourHope.com

Notes

For bonuses go to www.BelieveYourHope.com

Notes

Chapter 2

Believe in Your Power and Authority

2

I'm certain that as human beings, we're all believers. We may sometimes believe differently based on our culture, ethnic group, country of origin, or religion. We may also believe in someone else more than ourselves. However, the fact that we wake up every morning and talk, walk, eat, drive, and so on proves that we do those things because we believe we can do them. It demonstrates that we all have the capacity to act on faith.

What does that mean? Since you know you're a believer, what you do is a simple question of choice. You can choose to believe in your God-given power and authority, or you can continue to believe in the efficacy of your habits. The bottom line is that if you're looking for a major change in your life, you must first modify your beliefs to get a better lifestyle and accomplish your dreams.

When I was homeless, the situation wasn't easy; it was tough. Nonetheless, my belief system kept my hope and my smile alive. Maya Angelou once said, "It is belief in a power larger than myself and other than myself which allows me to venture into the unknowable." Sometimes, you need to be a little bit unrealistic. It's easy to believe in what you can see and touch, but you need faith to believe in things of the spirit and things that have yet to happen. What's known today was unknown yesterday, often because of someone's belief and faith. Consequently, I say that if you want to become the person you want to be and have those things you've been dreaming of for so long, you must update your belief system. Specifically, you need to first believe in yourself and then believe that everything is possible.

It's true—you were born with authority and power. Among millions of sperm, you were the only one who survived, and *The Bible* says God created you in his image and blessed you to rule on the earth. All you need to do is believe it yourself.

Jesus Christ, the greatest master who ever walked the earth, once said, "Everything is possible if you just believe." So believe in possibilities.

When you start believing in yourself and your power and authority, drastic changes will begin to happen in your life. But to really believe in yourself, you need to start changing your thought process. No matter what happens, you must think you're a winner, not a loser. A success, not a failure. A victor, not a victim. Stop and think about this for a moment: You were born free, wealthy, a prince or princess. Your birth brought joy to your family and the world, and you were a blessing to your mom and dad. Don't let anybody tell you anything less than that.

As a prince or princess, everything was ready for you before coming to this world—dresses, a bed, food, layettes, everything. Children tend to believe that everything's possible. You have big dreams. You compare yourself to the heroes and superstars you know. However, we live in a corrupt world of fake opinions and false information. And as you grow and learn, you begin to bend according to the beliefs of your parents, friends, schools, religions, and people around you. It's challenging to balance all these opinions. Confusion ensues, and you start canceling the dreams you had as a kid. You thought you were limitless, but now you see impossibilities instead of possibilities.

God, your creator, is waiting for you. So believe in God, yourself, and your dreams. The reality is that no one can believe for you; you've got to believe for yourself. After that, you can achieve anything you want to achieve!

I believe that nothing can stop you but yourself. Buddha once said, "All that we are is the result of what we have thought." That suggests you've reached the perfect moment to change your unbelief to belief and your doubt to faith. It's true: the time to update your belief in your power is today, not tomorrow.

And here's a critical piece of information: **What you think about the most is what leads your beliefs and life. So, change your thinking to change the results you get.**

The world moves because of people who believe in themselves, their ideas, and their God-given power. Their beliefs give them strength and quell their fear, which makes them willing to risk themselves and their lives, families, and money. They're the leaders in churches, businesses, industries, technologies, and politics.

Henry Ford wanted to create a V8 engine and believed it was possible. But he didn't know how to make it himself. So, he called on his top engineer to create a group of engineers to design the engine. The project had perplexed the engineers for a year when they came to Ford and declared that making a V8 was impossible. However, Mr. Ford believed so strongly in his idea of the V8 that he told them to continue working until they produced the engine. Forced by Ford's desire and belief, the engineers had no other choice but to continue until the day, like a miracle, it came to pass that they produced that V8 motor. You see, believing doesn't mean that what you envision will come easy; you're sure to meet with obstacles and unbelievers, and only tenacity will make the invisible visible.

> *"Man is not the creature of circumstances; circumstances are the creatures of men."*
> **– Benjamin Disraeli, British Prime Minister**

Let me state that idea in several ways:

- The person you are today results from your beliefs and actions yesterday.
- Hold onto your current beliefs, and you'll continue to get the same results you're experiencing today.
- If you don't like the circumstances you live in today, you must first change your beliefs and actions.
- I believe it was Albert Einstein who said that insanity is doing the same thing over and over and expecting different results.

Do you like the way you're living today? Would you like to continue living like that for the rest of your life? If the answer is no to either question, it's time to change your beliefs. Why can I make such a declaration? Science and history have shown that our actions are primarily driven by our beliefs.

Change is hard, but the world will move without you if you don't change yourself. I remember the first car I drove had a radio. Then the car industry began to put cassette players in all vehicles. After many years of using cassettes, they moved on to the CD player. Many drivers complained about the change, but there wasn't anything they could do except adapt. And now, the car factories have removed CD players and added Bluetooth, Sirius radio, USB ports, and Apple and Android car play. When the world changes, what will you do?

Everything is Risky

While it's true that "everything is risky," I don't say this to make you fearful but to get your attention. All things built by human hands can go awry, but the common belief is that they're safe to use. For example, most people believe it's safe to drive a car, fly in an airplane, cruise on the sea, drop from an aircraft with a parachute, or walk in the street because a light changes from green to red. The truth is that all those things present significant risk factors, but most people don't care; they choose to believe in their safety without questioning. How strange that we find it easier to believe in the safety of a stranger's invention than to believe in ourselves.

I understand that after living with a particular belief for many years, the risk represented by change might seem overwhelming. Still, I know the best bet you can make is believing in yourself, your power, and your ability to accomplish anything you want for a better life.

Yes, I promote the power of believing, but I realize it isn't easy for the average person to use that power in their favor. And as I mentioned, it's much easier to believe in what you can see and touch than to believe in yourself. I think that's why Abraham Lincoln once said, "To believe in the things you can see and touch is no belief at all, but to believe in the unseen is a triumph and a blessing." Enforcing your belief system takes hard work, training, and time. And when you spend years living with a consciousness of limitation, poverty, and weakness, it takes even more effort to switch your beliefs. Therefore, you must start from a place where you understand that it's possible and okay to update your beliefs, then constantly strive to believe more and more in your potential until you change your life forever. After all, if you can't believe in yourself, who else do you think will believe in you?

I'm convinced there's hope for anyone who wants to live a superior life by using the power of believing. So, in the coming chapters, I promise to elaborate on the practical side of this incredible power.

>*"Fear not, for I am with you;*
>*Be not dismayed, for I am your God.*
>*I will strengthen you, yes, I will help you,*
>*I will uphold you with my righteous right hand."*
>**(Isaiah 41:10)**

www.BelieveYourHope.com

Notes

For bonuses go to www.BelieveYourHope.com

Notes

Chapter 3

Your Intention Is Powerful

3

Once you arrive at the belief that you have power and authority, you may need to ask yourself, "What are my intentions?" Because power and authority are of no value if you have no intention of using them or don't know how to apply them in your daily life.

In his book *The Strangest Secret*, Earl Nightingale said, "We become what we think about." Based on that powerful assumption, I believe monitoring your thinking habits is vital. Moreover, to fulfill your intention, you must find and learn better ways to manipulate and focus your thoughts. I think the answers to the following questions can help to put you on the right path:

What is it that you want to become?

What do you think about the most every day?

When I was homeless in 2013, despite the darkness before me, my number one intention was to keep my joy no matter what. Consequently, I worked extremely hard to encourage myself to keep my smile and hopes alive. I read *The Bible* from cover to cover and devoured hundreds of books. The selective information I found in those books helped me focus and think about my intentions regarding myself, my family, and the people around me.

Today, I'm extremely happy and intend to show you shortcuts to help you polish your own intentions to create a happier life for yourself. You certainly don't have to go through all I did on the street. I believe it's my duty to write this book of hope, share the information I used successfully, and offer a coaching system for those who need extra help.

Life Will Test Your Intentions

At the beginning of 2002, I became part of a business network marketing organization that raised a lot of hope and made many promises. One of these promises was that someone could make a great deal of money and become financially free if they were willing to work very hard. I believed that promise and quickly applied myself. I was highly excited, so while going to college, I worked every day in that business, calling people, making appointments, and presenting the opportunity to everyone I could reach.

June came around, and even though I was eight credits away from getting my AA degree from Miami Dade College, the dream of financial freedom led me to drop out. However, I held onto my intention of returning to school to finish what I started and eventually obtain a bachelor's degree.

Many years passed, and I still regularly said, "I intend to get a bachelor's degree, and I will get it." In 2012, I registered and returned to school, only to drop out mid-semester. My intention still didn't waver, so after four more years, in December 2018, I registered at FIU and was accepted.

I took three classes in the first semester. My professors assigned homework and many chapters of reading in the first week! I thought I had made a mistake in returning to school and found myself thinking of dropping out again. After 16 years out of school, each assigned chapter seemed like a small book to me. I was devastated and afraid I couldn't pass those classes while working full-time at my day job. Negative thoughts and words started a war between my intention and beliefs. The battle was so intense that I couldn't sleep for about two weeks.

The problem was that even though my intention was to get my degree, I believed that I had made a mistake and wouldn't be able to pass. Good thing my intention was so laser-focused on getting that bachelor's degree! I woke up in the middle of the night with a little voice from within saying, "Alex, you can do it," and I repeated out loud, "I can do it." From that moment, I followed my intention with the belief that I could do it, and two years and four months later, I graduated with a bachelor's degree in communication.

Of course, easy wasn't an option; university sorely tested me. But I remained so focused on my intention that sleepless nights were no match. To work long, full-time hours, care for my family, and at the same time dare to get a degree was tough, but I did it. Achievement takes hard work, intense focus, and determination to follow your intention.

For bonuses go to ...

What You Think About the Most Will Feed Your Intention

Based on the Law of Attraction, you attract what you think about the most. Therefore, you should remember that your thinking and beliefs always play with your intention; it's challenging to deal with the world and still hold onto your pure intention. I believe this is where millions fail because the world is so busy and disturbing that they get distracted. Too many things happen with your friends and family and on TV and social media. You can lose your intention in the storm before you know it. Therefore, I believe it's imperative to track your thoughts at every moment—if you're serious about keeping up with your intentions.

Self-Discipline is Required to Maintain Your Intention

I am sort of a skinny guy, and my intention is to keep it that way for the rest of my life. I remember a time at work when one of my co-workers said, "Hey, Alex, how do you stay the way you are—so fit, so skinny?"

I told him, "I don't just stay the way I am; It's my intention to keep that way forever."

"How do you do it?"

"You know, many people—even if they weren't programmed to eat—can't resist the temptation when there's food around, especially if it's free food. So they eat. My number one intention is not to eat when there is food around. I eat what I'm programmed to eat, when I want to eat, and where I want to eat. That's my discipline. I control my eating habits."

It's important not to let peer pressure and the world convince you to deviate from focusing on your intention. Be disciplined. Be focused. Because at the end of the day, you're the only person responsible for leading your intention.

If you intend to do good, your thoughts and results will tend to be good. On the other hand, if you intend to do wrong, your thoughts will be bad, and so will your results. You drive your life, so the destination you're heading for is based on your intention or lack thereof. You have the ultimate power to choose and balance your intention. It will determine your actions, and your actions determine the results. Success in a nutshell.

"For as he thinks in his heart, so is he."
(Proverbs 23-7)

Remember that your intentions create emotions that generate thoughts which drive your actions. Those behaviors define you, your success, or your failure.

Let's say you own an airplane, and one day you go flying with no destination in mind; you have no intention. Where do you think you'll end up? Maybe nowhere. Maybe in the ocean. Maybe on the side of a mountain. Who knows?

Your life will follow your intention. Everything that has happened in your life—good or bad—has followed that intention. If it's based on hate, then every idea coming into your mind will help you to fulfill that hateful intention. Alternatively, if you intend to love, only good ideas will come to you. You're the master of your destiny!

Saint Augustin once said in one of his predications, "Love and do what you will." I believe he said that because if you love, you can't do anything harmful.

And in a Bible story (I believe it's in Mark 12:28-30), one of the Pharisees was trying to challenge Jesus and asked him, "Of all the commandments, which is the most important?"

Jesus answered, "The most important one, love the Lord your God with all your heart and soul and with all your mind and strength. The second is to love your neighbor as yourself."

So, you can understand just how strong LOVE is if you intend to do good for yourself, your family, neighbors, city, country, and the world. I truly believe that love is the greatest intention you can cultivate because it guides all others.

Love is patient. Love is persistent. Love is joy. Love is comfort. Love is happiness. So, intend to love and meld all other intentions with that love.

www.BelieveYourHope.com

Notes

For bonuses go to www.BelieveYourHope.com

Notes

Chapter 4

If You Know What You Want, You Can Get It

4

"Ask, and you will be given what you ask for.
Seek, and you will find.
Knock, and the door will be opened."
(Matthew 7:7)

The universe is limitless and full of abundance. However, it's up to you to select what you want. No one will give you everything you want, but neither can they stop you from getting those things. God has given you the power to choose and create the lifestyle you want for yourself and your family. The fact is that almost everything you want is already in existence. If it isn't, you have the power to create it.

The main question is, "Do I know what I really want?" Most of the time, people think they know what they want but keep their minds on what they need. That means it's crucial to differentiate between needs and wants. The dictionary explains that a "need" is a necessity, something you must have for a satisfactory life, while a "want" is a hope or desire to possess or do something.

To better understand, let's consider hunger. If you're hungry, you need food. But if you desire or choose to eat a particular

For bonuses go to ...

food to satisfy that hunger, I'm sure you can agree we're no longer talking about need but have wandered into the realm of want. Consequently, I can say that to fulfill a want, you must know exactly what that want is.

One of my best experiences regarding knowing what you want occurred a few months ago. I was talking with one of my older sisters on the phone. She was excited about a project she was working on and put me on hold.

When my sister returned, she said, "Listen, I'm driving with Joe (one of my nephews), and he has suggested I ask you to buy a bedroom set for Mom."

I said, "Really?"

She answered, "Yes."

So I asked, "How much does it cost?"

She exclaimed, "What?!" and remained silent for a while.

I asked, "What just happened?"

She answered, "I didn't believe I would get that answer from you. Wow! You've changed my way of thinking completely." Then, she continued, "I don't know how much it costs. Let me check that out, and I will let you know."

My sister had a good intention. However, she didn't know what bedroom furniture she wanted to buy for my mom. Mom has six children, of which I am the fourth. I was ready at any moment to buy the bedroom set for my mother, no matter the price, and without the help of my five siblings. But how could I do that without correct knowledge?

It took my sister more than two weeks to get back to me.

She called me from a furniture store and said, "I found a beautiful set."

I said, "Great, do you really like it for Mom?"

"Yes, but it's a little bit expensive."

"Okay, how much is it?"

She told me the price, but I could hear some hesitation in her voice.

I asked her, "When would you like to get it?"

"Now."

"Okay."

After a while, my sister acted scared and said, "Listen, I was wrong. The store manager now tells me the price is $500 more than I reported earlier."

I said, "Okay, do you want the money now?"

"Of course. Yes!"

And with just a click, I sent the money to her through Zelle.

You see, it wasn't a lack of money that kept me from buying the bedroom set for my mother. I was ready the first day my sister mentioned it. The problem was that she didn't know exactly what she wanted. In the end, it was a blessing for me to be able to do that for Mom; I was full of joy knowing that she could sleep better and be happier. My point? When you have a burning desire for something, know precisely what you want from the universe, and understand you must focus on that goal, it will come to you faster than you can imagine.

Another time, one of my younger brothers approached me and said, "Alex, help me find a job. I've been looking at many places but can't find anything."

"What do you mean that you're looking everywhere?"

"I sent my resumé everywhere, but no one called me!"

"Of course, no one will call you because you don't know

what you want."

"But I told you that I'm looking for a job."

"Exactly! You're looking for a job but don't know what job. Nor do you know what company you would like to work for."

"I would like to work for Marshall."

"Now you're talking. Which Marshall would you like to work for?"

"The one in downtown Miami."

"Have you ever visited that Marshall?"

My brother nodded and said that he had.

Hearing that, I said, "Now, you're going to visit that store with purpose. Go there, walk around, and study the behavior of every employee. Return and do the same thing as often as necessary, and when you feel comfortable enough, get dressed up and take action. But don't ask for an application; instead, ask for the manager. When the manager comes, give him a firm handshake, and say that you've come to help him get a better store with better customer service."

My brother did what I suggested, and the company hired him. Before long, they promoted him to assistant manager and then manager. Moreover, the last time I checked, he was being celebrated with a special jacket from the Marshall corporation as the best manager in his district.

Keep Your Desire Alive No Matter What

I developed the thinking I taught my brother during my time as a homeless person. It became a habit to focus on what I wanted instead of the misery of my living conditions. As a result, once we were able to rent an apartment, I said to myself, "I want to have a new car. I want a big house with more space than I can use. I want to return to school and get a bachelor's degree in communication. And then I want to write a book." There were some delays because I didn't know the process to follow to get what I wanted. But I was willing to learn. I read hundreds of books (you name it, I read it), revisited the notes I took from many seminars and conferences, and even read *The Bible* from cover to cover.

I was hungry and constantly looked for the correct information. I knew I could get anything I wanted, but finding the way was up to me. And as I digested the collected data, certain commonalities emerged. I began to make sense of myself, applied some of what I learned, and experienced positive results. In the end, I accomplished each of the desires identified while homeless.

You see, it doesn't matter where you are today or what you're doing; the fact remains that if you have a burning desire and really know what you want, you'll get it. I believe there's no dream too big for you to achieve. It all depends on the way you think. If you think you can, you can; if you think you can't, you can't. Many people thought that a Black man couldn't become the president of the United States of America; however, Barack Obama came with a burning desire, a belief that he could do it, and the motto, *Yes We Can.* He became president and was re-elected to run for president again! The moral of the story is that there's no excuse for not making the changes you want in your life because everything is possible and within reach.

For bonuses go to ...

> *"If you are falling, make sure that you fall on your back because if you can look up, you can stand up."*
> **– Les Brown**

The Power of Unity

Sometimes, there are many things that you want to happen or have or do, but you can't accomplish them by yourself. As such, finding people to align with and agree with and who believe in you becomes essential.

According to *The Bible*, after the great flood destroyed everything, the earth was of one language and speech. In time, the generations following Noah devised a plan to build a city and tower whose top would reach unto heaven. Nowadays, many people would say that's impossible, but Genesis 11:6 reports that God said, "If as one people speaking the same language they have begun to do this, then nothing they plan to do will be impossible for them."

God, the creator of everything in the universe, says that when a group of people really need something and believe in the possibility, they'll get it. I've seen it for myself. So many miracles and achievements happen when an organization wants to do, get, or have something, and everyone in that organization agrees to work together to make it come to pass.

It was in mid-2011 that I became conscious of the power of unity. After reading Napoleon Hill's *Think & Grow Rich*, I created a mastermind group with one of my brothers-in-law and another family member. The three of us lived in Miami, Florida, but my brother-in-law wasn't yet a legal immigrant in the United States. He had applied to become a legal resident quite a while before and hadn't received any communication from US Immigration. So, one day when we each asked what it was that we most wanted, my brother said, "I want to know where I stand legally, and I want to have a notice from US immigration." Our rules were that all three of us agree on an issue, apply the "get what you want steps," and pray about it. You may find it unbelievable, but three days later, the first piece of mail he found in his mailbox was a letter from Immigration. We were excited and grateful to see how quickly the power of unity worked.

Miracles Happen When a Team Works in Unity

One month when I worked as a car salesman in a dealership, upper management challenged the sales group to sell 200 new cars. Moreover, everyone would receive a considerable bonus if the dealership reached that goal. The catch was that we didn't have 200 vehicles on the ground. Consequently, almost every salesman and saleswoman was pessimistic at the beginning of the month.

About mid-month, the general sales manager (GSM) came up with an idea and called everyone to a meeting. He gave us a piece of paper on which he had printed the number 200. Then he said, "I want you to put that on your desk, and for the rest of the month, it's what we're going to talk about, and it's what we're going to focus on." Some people didn't believe we could do it, but we kept selling.

For bonuses go to ...

I remember we were missing a couple of cars on the last day of the month, and one saleswoman came to me and said, "Alex, do you think we'll reach that 200 cars?"

I thought about it for a minute and answered, "Yes! Because we have more than 30 people thinking and working with each other to reach that goal."

Then, as I was crossing the salesroom, I saw another saleswoman sitting sadly with her hand on her face. So I asked her, "Why are you sitting like that?"

She said, "You know we aren't going to reach those 200 cars."

"Don't worry," I told her. "Everything is going to be all right."

Sometime between 6:30 and 7:00 PM that day, the GSM called everyone to a meeting at the sales desk. He came in with his face drooping down, and the saleswoman who had been so sad said, "The way his face looks, I don't believe we made it."

I replied, "I'm sure we made it."

The GSM said, "You know, sometimes you're looking for something and working very hard to get it, and you fail. But that isn't our case because we were looking for 200 cars, and we sold 204 new cars."

Everyone clapped in complete joy. Then, the saleswoman who had been so sad began to jump and hit me on my back by saying, "Alex, we got it because of you, because of your faith. You have faith!"

Yes, indeed, I had faith. However, I believe we sold those cars and got the bonus because everybody worked together toward it.

www.BelieveYourHope.com

When You Really Know What You Want, Others Will Follow You

I have a story about a great man, an outstanding new priest in Miami, Florida. His name is Reginald Jean-Mary. Shortly after becoming a priest, he was promoted to administrator of the parish of the Notre Dame d'Haiti church in Miami. The parishioners had been attending mass in an old building unsuitable for a church community. Consequently, with the approval of the head of the Catholic Church in Miami, he decided to construct a new building for Notre Dame d'Haiti.

Despite the agreement with his superior, this priest didn't have any money to start the project, but he did have a burning desire for progress, and his dream was very much alive. So he forged ahead and presented the idea to his parishioners. They were all for it, and the prospect of fundraising the millions of dollars needed to start the building filled them with excitement and joy. The priest was all in and worked day and night, creating different fundraising movements to achieve their goal.

The path wasn't easy. For example, the congregation had a sizeable treed lot, but the trees were hundreds of years old. Based on that fact, the city of Miami opposed the build, saying the trees couldn't be removed because they were national patrimonies. After many failed negotiations, the priest presented the fact to the parishioners, and they began to send notes to the elected officials. The next step was to gather before the city hall to manifest their unhappiness and protest the officials' decision. Their protestations continued almost daily to build more pressure on the top officials.

For bonuses go to ...

Ultimately, the dream was bigger than the resistance, and the city gave the green light to cut the trees and build the church. **A large enough dream can overcome any resistance.** The priest started with just an idea, which became a dream for many. He didn't have the money to build the church; however, bringing the parishioners into the dream generated the money and won one of the biggest challenges against the city of Miami. Consequently, they were able to build the Church of Notre Dame d'Haiti.

Even though your goal may seem impossible, God will always make a way and is always there to help. But it's up to you to decide what you want, and no one will start the journey for you. Just know that when you have a burning desire to get something in life, ideas and opportunities will always come your way. The first step is deciding what you really want for yourself and your family.

So, what *do* you want?

www.BelieveYourHope.com

Notes

For bonuses go to www.BelieveYourHope.com

Notes

Chapter 5

Set Your Goals

5

Once you understand and believe you're a powerful human with highly positive intention and know what you want to have a pleasant life, it's time to set your goals.

Setting goals is essential for building the desires of your heart and achieving your dreams. I know you'll have heard this before, but I can't emphasize it enough: You must be committed to setting goals if you're serious about getting what you want. Goal setting helps you to focus on your target. Certainly, everybody can wish to have nice things or go to exciting places. However, the individual committed to a specific plan is far more likely to achieve their objective.

> *"Setting goals is the first step in*
> *turning the invisible into the visible."*
> **– Tony Robbins**

I say your hope can become a reality because I know it's possible to achieve anything you think about when you set specific goals and work to achieve them. It's simple! Let's say that you want to build a house. Will you call an architect or an engineer and tell him, "Just build me a house?" Of course not. I'm confident you'll give the engineer all the specifications for your desired house. He'll also need to know where you want to build the house, what shape you want it to be, the number and placement of bathrooms, as well as how many rooms you want, their size, and their purpose.

Contrary to popular belief, it's not enough to have a burning desire to get something. You must also set goals, plan your actions, and carry them out. Your goal is to get what you want, but to activate that thing—turning it from the invisible to the visible—you must fully describe the details of your plan to achieve your dream. You must be specific, and you must act on your plan!

> *"Stop setting goals. Goals are pure fantasy unless you have a specific plan to achieve them."*
> **– Stephen Covey**

To better understand, let's consider that you have a car. You open it, get in, and sit. But you don't turn the ignition key. Where will you be after one hour? You'll be sitting right where you started. The same holds for goal setting. You won't get anywhere if you set a goal but don't have a plan for reaching it. It's just a vague wish.

The first thing you have to do is to put your goal in writing. Then you need to plan the path you'll follow to get there. Moreover, you must be confident that your plan will lead you to your goal. Having a date for when your dream will become a reality is also crucial. Most people won't take action unless there's the pressure of a deadline. I would even go so far as to suggest that you make yourself accountable to someone—to keep you honest! Because even if you do everything perfectly, your success depends on your work ethic and how well you focus on your goals.

What happens if you experience some delays? It's all good. Just be aware of what you did right and what you did wrong, then reset and replan. The main idea is to keep moving toward your goal no matter what you encounter along the way. Be willing to change your plan as necessary, but never take your focus off your goal.

One last suggestion. If your goal isn't big enough to energize you to wake up every day and motivate you to keep moving with joy in your heart, then it's time to change the goal.

In the movie *King Richard* (based on a true story), Richard Williams, the father of Venus and Serena Williams, had a goal he translated into a plan for his two daughters. He wanted his two daughters to become the best tennis players in the world. To take that goal from invisible to visible, he wrote a plan of about 78 pages and followed it with his daughters.

Williams became their trainer, practicing with them every day and constantly injecting into their minds the idea of becoming the two best tennis players in the world. Today, the Williams sisters are just that. And their achievements aren't a coincidence. Venus and Serena are proof that setting your goals, planning to achieve them, and following that plan is the way to achieve your dreams.

You can't build a safe, reliable, and quality skyscraper without a certified plan. Nor can you reach your goals without a plan for how you'll get there.

I think it's wise for you to understand that when pursuing your dream, easy won't be an option. Things might even be scary at times. So always be ready and willing to deal with obstacles and objections. You should also expect that following the plan that leads to your goals will require much time, money, and effort. But if your goal is big enough, nothing will stop you.

For example, when I had to go back to school and get myself a major in communication, there were many hurdles. I had to drop out in 2012, and it wasn't until six years later that I was accepted and registered at Florida International University.

When the first professor arrived, he said, "Read chapters one through four." In my second class, the professor said, "Read chapters one, two, and three." My third professor said, "You're to read chapters one to three." There was homework for all three classes!

Within the first week, I was thinking about dropping out. I couldn't sleep. I was overwhelmed. And I thought that I had made a serious mistake returning to school; it was just too much to handle. Except ... one sleepless night, a little voice from within said, "Alex, you can do this. You can handle it. Go for it!"

Quite suddenly, I felt at peace, so I kept on moving. I'm eternally grateful because, in April of 2021, I graduated with a bachelor's degree. I worked full-time, accrued no student loans, made time for my family, and still graduated! You may disagree, but it seems an extraordinary accomplishment to me. So, I'm telling you that if you have a goal, an excellent plan to support it, and you keep moving toward your final destination no matter what comes your way, you'll achieve that goal. I believe this so strongly that I'm unafraid to say you can take it to the bank because it will work every time, all the time.

Once again, if you have a goal, an excellent plan to support it, and you keep moving toward that goal no matter what comes your way, you'll achieve it!

For bonuses go to www.BelieveYourHope.com

Notes

Chapter 6

Imagination Will Lead You to Your Destination

6

"Imagination is more important than knowledge."
– Albert Einstein

What's Knowledge Without Imagination?

Most of your knowledge today is based on the imagination and actions of someone who came before you. You know about airplanes because of the imagination of the Wright brothers. You use light bulbs because Thomas Edison imagined the incandescent bulb and then created it. You enjoy beautiful modern outfits, different brands of cars, and a house packed with various furniture designs because someone imagined those articles and invested time, labor, and money to create them. Other than the natural things God created, all you see and touch began in someone's imagination.

And I have great news for you. It's time to get your hopes up because the "imagine nation" hasn't ended. It's alive and well, and it's limitless. Your place in that splendid country is secure, so you can begin imagining a new lifestyle immediately.

For bonuses go to ...

What is Imagination?

Based on the Merriam-Webster dictionary, "Imagination is the act or power of forming a mental image of something not present to the senses or never before wholly perceived in reality." I assure you, we each have the capacity to imagine. And while God created us as co-creators and rulers, imagination is the only way to activate and fulfill that power.

Everything is Created Twice

Whatsoever is—if you can see, touch, and sense it, then it was fabricated or created twice. The chair you're sitting in first appeared in the thoughts of someone who shaped it mentally and then constructed it in physical form to be commercialized and used by others. Whether it's the outfit you're wearing, the car you're driving, the house you're living in, or the plate you're eating from, each was created twice. Because nothing happens until someone thinks about it, imagines it, feels it, and makes it. Thought first, creation second!

The Most Powerful Miracle in the Universe

Every machine, computer system, and electronic device has a limit, but the brain is limitless. You can create virtually anything with your brain and the proper use of imagination.

Maybe someone can put you in jail, use you as a slave, or

even stop you from taking specific actions, but no one can stop you from imagining the scenario of your choice. I remember Les Brown, one of the greatest public speakers in the world, recounting the story of a boy who needed to see something in a window. However, someone pressed his head whenever he tried to stand up to watch. After a while, the boy said, "It's okay that you're pressing my head; I can still see it in my mind." The boy disregarded the obstacle and saw what he wished to see. You have the same capacity to visualize whatever you want, and no one in the world can stop you.

When I was homeless, I had two choices: to believe in the misery of the moment or to hope for what I could create through my imagination. I chose the second option. And while I worked through the tough times, I used my imagination to create the lifestyle I have today. First, the mental, then the physical.

What's Your Potential?

God gave us all the potential we need to create and live a happy life. However, many people go through their entire lives without using the power of their imagination.

For example, when you go to school, they teach you using books written by other people. And let's say you did great at school and graduated. You're happy. Everybody in your family is happy.

Next, you send your resume to a company and get hired. But you can't just start working. First, you're assigned a supervisor who guides you and instructs what to do. You do exactly what they tell you to do, and you do it for 30 years in a row, then you retire. Terrific!

Except you spent your life applying other people's ideas and imagination—from school to the professional level. Did you employ your potential?

Elevate Your Thinking Habits

I believe it was Wallace D. Wattles, in *The Science of Getting Rich,* who wrote, "To think health when surrounded by the appearances of disease or to think riches when in the midst of appearances of poverty, requires power; but he who acquires this power becomes a MASTER MIND. He can conquer fate; he can have what he wants." Yes, indeed, you can have whatever you want; however, you need to elevate your thinking habits to do that.

I understand that most of your thoughts and emotions occur in the subconscious mind, which can't tell the imagined from reality. How scary! Thoughts and emotions you have no conscious access to are driving your behavior. Do you get the importance of this idea? When you visualize something or otherwise focus your thoughts, they can become a reality in your life. Therefore, I would tell you to be careful about what you think.

Napoleon Hill, in *Think and Grow Rich,* stated that "Thoughts are things." Consequently, I consider thoughts to be concrete and believe you need to learn to focus them on what you want to do and what you want to happen in your life. But beware, creative, positive, and objective thinking are far from easy because of the constant movement of the world around us. It takes commitment and hard work to create a habit of thinking differently than you used to; there will be a battlefield in your mind.

The Bible says, "Resist the devil, and he will flee." So, if whatever keeps you from thinking about your heart's desires and dreams is the devil, you must resist. And if you want to achieve something, you need to think about it so much that you can start seeing it with your mind's eye. Do that, and the thing is already yours.

Visualization is Divine

Imagine if car manufacturers, house builders, boat constructors, and airplane manufacturers began to do things without visualizing them first or knowing precisely what they intended to do. What do you think would happen to the world? I believe global chaos and disorder would ensue.

Our creator is a God of order, which is why He created the universe in an orderly manner. God said, "Let there be light, and there was light." Do you think He had the image of light in his mind and knew exactly how it would look? Certainly! And as a co-creator, He gave you the same power to keep the world in order while you create whatever you envision; God created us with the capacity to see things in our minds before transforming them into matter.

God told Abraham, "I will surely bless you and make your

For bonuses go to ...

descendants as numerous as the stars in the sky and as the sand on the seashore." If you try to understand the previous sentence, you'll realize that God gave Abraham the image of the blessings that would come upon him. Now, let's pretend you have a green apple that you bought for 50 cents and intend to resell for one dollar. How many green apples do you have to sell if you want to make a profit of ten dollars? If you can see that green apple in your mind, envision the profit from one apple, and find the answer to my question, you're already on your way to success.

$100,000 Discount

One of my co-workers told me she had a house, but there was another house she really liked that was only a couple of blocks away from her. One day, she was passing by, and that particular house was on the market for sale. She tried to convince her husband to buy the house; however, her husband claimed the price of over half a million dollars was too much.

Nevertheless, the woman didn't give up. Instead, she got a picture of that house and put it in her closet. She told me that she looked at the photograph every day, then closed her eyes and visualized living in it. The house was eventually pulled off the market, but my co-worker kept imagining that she owned it. About two years later, the couple went and knocked on the door of her dream house and asked the owner if he still wanted to sell the house. He said, "Yes!" That excited them, so they asked the owner about the price. It was almost one hundred thousand dollars lower than the previous asking price. They bought the house for four hundred and fifty-seven thousand dollars.

If You Can See It Mentally, Then You Can Have It Physically

Keep it simple. Visualization or imagination isn't complicated; it's part of our nature to visualize. For example, if you're at home right now, can you close your eyes for a couple of seconds and see—in your mind—a picture of your office or workstation? Now, can you see one of your co-workers standing next to you? Congratulations! That was visualization, and you did it. If you can do that simple exercise, you're in an excellent position to begin your success journey. You just have to channel your thinking and visualize what you want to have or happen.

Something I believe can help you with visualizing is creating a dream board. A dream board is an empty board where you write down all your dreams and then attach pictures of what you want to have or accomplish. To activate your board, make sure you put it in a place where you can see it daily. Take three to five minutes to look at your board each day, then close your eyes and see yourself in possession of what you want to have or do. Enjoy the moment because you're on your way to success.

For bonuses go to ...

Enjoy Then, So That You Can Enjoy Now

One day—I remember it was the last day of a month—I was passing in front of the dealership and saw a salesman stressing out. I asked him how he was doing, and he told me he needed to sell one more car to get his bonus.

"Why do you want to make that bonus?"

"I need the money to save because we're planning to buy a house."

"Should you sell that car, how would you celebrate your success?"

"I would go and enjoy a lobster."

"Where would you like to go to eat that lobster?"

"A Red Lobster restaurant."

"Okay, but would you go by yourself or invite someone else?"

"You know what? I would like it delivered to my house."

"Would you eat it in the dining room or your bedroom?"

" I have an office in my room. I will eat there."

"Congratulations!"

"Why?"

"The sale you needed is already done. And you've celebrated with a delicious plate from Red Lobster. So, just wait. The customer will show, and that car will be delivered."

I went my way after that. But I was crossing the showroom an hour later and saw him sitting and negotiating with a customer. He made the sale! After completing his delivery, he came to me and said, "Thank you, Alex. Your system is working. Sell it, celebrate it, and it will be sold."

www.BelieveYourHope.com

***"Therefore I say unto you, what things soever ye desire,
when ye pray, believe that ye receive them,
and ye shall have them."***
(Mark 11: 24)

As a disclaimer, I would say that there's no exact time when you'll accomplish your goals. It depends on the level of focus you place on your dreams and the time you invest in visualization. However, one thing I know is that if you keep visualizing your dreams and working toward them, you'll accomplish them.

For bonuses go to www.BelieveYourHope.com

Notes

Chapter 7

The Power of Your Words

7

*"A man's stomach will be satisfied with the fruit of his mouth.
He will be satisfied with the consequence of his words.
Death and life are in the power of the tongue.
And those who love it, indulge it, will eat its fruit and
bear the consequences of their words."*
(Proverbs 18:20-21)

So far, you've read that you're a powerful human being who can manage your intentions, set your goals, and visualize the realization of your dreams. However, while achieving those goals and dreams, you still must deal with daily issues and what's happening in the world around you—one that's increasingly bombarded with noise and opinions. That's why you need to know how to use your words correctly. Because what you say can either help or deter you from your objective. More details follow to give you a better understanding that your words are one of the most powerful weapons in your possession.

Be careful with your words. They're like a sharp, two-edged knife.

With your words, you can:

- Bless and curse
- Elevate and degrade
- Talk about love and hate
- Construct and destroy
- Bring honey and bitterness

It's true! You can alternatively build your success and destroy your accomplishments with words. Therefore, it's imperative that you take great care in what you choose to say.

Nothing Happens Until Someone Says Something

Imagine you're in love with a beautiful woman but never talked to her about your feelings. How can you hope to see that love returned?

When you visit your doctor, and they ask you how you're feeling or why you came to see them, isn't it true that the words you choose help the doctor to put together a plan of healing for you?

Your words impact all aspects of your life. For example, no one will know about or understand your purpose until you learn to communicate what you want in a certain way, making it difficult for you to accomplish those goals.

God could have easily created everything without saying a word, but he chose to say, "Let there be light." And there was light! I believe he was teaching the human race that words are an essential part of creation. *The Bible* says, "Ask and it shall be given to you." How can you do that without formulating your words properly?

Words make this world go around. So, your lifestyle depends largely on the words you say or use every day.

Put Some Hope In Your Words

I believe the most extraordinary power you have is your God-given authority to choose; He gave you agency. For example, you can choose to use negative words or keep them straight and positive no matter what happens. It's entirely up to you.

I don't remember where I first heard this, but there's a saying, "If you have nothing good to say, then remain quiet." The lesson is that it's better to keep silent than to talk negatively about anyone (including yourself) because whatever you talk about, you also think and attract.

One of my co-workers complained that his business wasn't booming.

I asked him, "Why do you think there's a day and a night?"

He couldn't answer, so I said, "The day is for you to work and the night to sleep."

I continued to tell him that life is like a chain of mountains and that after every mountain, there's a valley.

He said, "What do you mean?"

For bonuses go to ...

"Life isn't a straight line. Sometimes there are highs and other times lows. None of them lasts forever. So instead of complaining, why don't you say that your business will boom? And repeat it several times throughout your day."

My co-worker did precisely that and sold a car a few hours later. I joked about it and said, "I rest my case!"

He laughed and said, "Thank you, Alex! Thank you."

**"For by your words you will be justified,
and by your words you will be condemned."
(Matthew 12:37)**

Be kind to yourself, your kids and family, and the people around you. Don't talk just for the sake of talking because your words can bring as much pain as joy. You would also be wise to think twice before opening your mouth to communicate anything. You see, not only does every word you utter have power, but all words are associated with corresponding images and feelings. If I say that you look beautiful or handsome, what do you think or feel? What if I say that you're ugly? How do you feel, and what do you think about me?

As you can imagine, a spoken word can change your life for good or bad. For instance, I met with one of my nieces at a family party a few days ago. I was happy to see her because we hadn't seen each other for quite a while. After greeting her warmly, I asked why she had never called me. She said, " I'm sorry, uncle, but I'm swamped. Besides, the last time I called you to say happy birthday, you told me it wasn't your birthday. I felt bad; it was hurtful." Wow! I didn't know that telling her the truth would hurt her feelings. You see, sometimes people won't tell you when you hurt them with your words or the tone of your voice. Instead, they simply stop talking to you.

If you're not careful, you'll not only hurt the people around you, but you may cause more self-damage than you could ever imagine possible.

Talk With Hope and Feed Your Subconscious Mind

Your subconscious mind is always listening, talking, and acting. Therefore, I believe it's extremely important to lead your subconscious mind in the right direction. The issue with the subconscious mind is that it doesn't know the difference between good and bad. Consequently, it works to bring whatever you talk about into reality.

I know that it's not easy to protect yourself from all you're exposed to, but you can protect yourself from yourself by consciously selecting the words you use for internal and external communication. If you talk with hope, your subconscious mind will help to attract hopeful results. But if you navigate with negative talk, your subconscious mind will work hard to bring you negative results. It's all about attraction, and your subconscious will help you to attract what you think and talk about the most. So talk with hope!

"Let the weak say, I am strong."
(Joel 3:10)

The world moves with significant repetition. The bus driver travels the same route daily. You start your car the same way every day, follow the same path to work, run the same errands, and return home. The supermarkets open and close on the same weekly schedule. Tires invariably roll. The fact is most everything you do and see is a repetition.

Let's make sure you understand the implications of repetition. You're living the way you do because of the words (and actions) you repeat daily. That means if you want to change your life, you'll need to change your habitual vocabulary (and actions). *The Bible* says that faith comes by hearing, so why not begin helping yourself by repeatedly listening to what's good, delightful, fruitful, and uplifting? Instead of saying things are worsening, repeat phrases like, "I believe things will get better because there's no night without day and no darkness without light." Repeatedly express your goals in a positive way because the more you do that, the more you'll find yourself in possession of what you want. Your words are powerful!

> ***"There is Power in Words.***
> ***What you say is What you Get."***
> ***– Zig Ziglar***

For argument's sake, imagine you can get whatever you want by saying what you want. What would you say? Would you say good things or bad things? Would you use positive or negative words? The issue here is that most people say things based on their experience, environment, beliefs, and the opinions of others. What it comes down to is that if you don't like how you're living today or want to enjoy a better life than what you have, you need to do something different—you need to change. The place to begin is changing the selection of words you use in your daily life.

> *"Whosoever shall say unto this mountain,*
> *be thou removed, and be thou cast into the sea,*
> *and shall not doubt in his heart,*
> *but shall believe that those things which he saith*
> *shall come to pass; he shall have whatsoever he saith."*
> **(Mark 11:23)**

I believe it's powerful to use positive words no matter what you face. For example, if you think the mountain you're facing is too big to be removed, you may be tempted to curse and condemn yourself using profanity. Use bad words, and you'll get bad results. However, make the positive choice to believe, and miracles can happen. Because the more you repeat a thing, and the more you believe in that thing, the more possibilities you have to see it manifest in your life.

Consequently, I would say to you that while it's tough not to talk about what you're enduring right now, the results will be sweeter if you can switch your thoughts and words to reflect what you want to happen in your life. Indeed, it's crucial to change your mindset if you want to achieve better results. A change of your words can help do that. Talk about how you want your life to be, not how it is.

What you're living today results from what you were talking about yesterday. It seems plausible that if you change the words you use now, you'll change how you think and behave. That course correction, though it seems insignificant at the start, will eventually bring you to a destination far removed from where you were originally headed.

> *"You see things; and you say why?*
> *But I dream things that never were; and I say why not?"*
> **– George Bernard Shaw**

So, if you want a life full of abundance, joy, and peace, say it repeatedly and unleash the power of your words.

Word By Word

Desmond Tutu once said, "There is only one way to eat an elephant, a bite at a time." I agree and believe it requires tons of work to activate the power within your words. But if you're hungry enough, you can start by training yourself—word by word.

There's a force, an image, a spirit hiding in every word you speak. So, don't talk just for the sake of talking. Instead, speak by choice and with purpose. And know what you're talking about because what you say will come to pass.

Let's say you want to be happier than you are. You can start by saying "Happy" and repeating it often throughout your day. Repeating the word happy both aloud and silently can help you regain your happiness. Moreover, to impress your subconscious mind, you can choose to stand in front of a mirror, look yourself straight in the eyes, repeat the word happy, and say to yourself, "I'm happy and happier than ever before." You can use this technique for anything you want to manifest in your life. Empower yourself, one word at a time!

For bonuses go to www.BelieveYourHope.com

Notes

Chapter 8

Gratitude

8

*"But blessed are your eyes because they see,
and your ears because they hear."*
(Matthew 13:16)

So far, you've read about many techniques to build hope and achieve your dreams:

- God created you in his image
- You're blessed
- You're a ruler with full power
- You have the choice to manage your intentions toward whatever you want.

However, to stay aligned with yourself, the universe, and your destiny, you must take stock of all your gifts and talents. One of the best ways to count these blessings is through gratitude.

Gratitude is the essence of life—the door which leads to infinite joy, contentment, abundance, success, prosperity, and humility. Gratitude is acknowledging where you come from with heartfelt thankfulness. Gratitude is taking account of all the

For bonuses go to ...

details that make you the person you are today and giving thanks for them. Gratitude is having an appreciation for everybody in your life, good or bad; gratitude for the good people who bring you love and joy and the haters who help you become strong. Gratitude is being thankful for what you have now and what you want to achieve.

Believe it or not, you have more than you think and are better than you think. Now, it's up to you to be grateful or ungrateful. Remember, you have full power, you're in total control, and you drive the car of your life. You can choose to go right or left, or you can stop. But no matter what you decide to do, always remember to be grateful.

There's a true story my wife has told me on countless occasions. The story is about a priest who thought he had a lot of problems in his congregation. He became depressed until one day when he couldn't keep it to himself anymore. The man called on another priest and told him he needed help. Then he asked the other priest if he was in his office at that moment.

The other priest said, "Yes, but I have a meeting with someone right now."

He replied, "No problem, I will come and wait."

The other priest thought, *That must be a serious problem!*

When the troubled priest arrived at the presbytery, the other priest was still in a meeting. Meanwhile, the visiting priest went into the chapel and waited there. Thinking that he was alone, the man started talking to God about his misery. He was utterly pessimistic about his situation and asked God why he had to endure so many problems.

Suddenly he heard a noise, looked back, and saw a man with no legs making his way through the chapel. The man began to pray out loud, saying, "Thank you, God, for the sickness I have. It allows me to come closer to you. I give thanks for not having legs because I have two hands and two eyes, and my brain is functioning perfectly. Thank you, God, that I can breathe. Thank you, thank you, thank you!"

After listening to the prayer of the amputated man, the priest realized he had much for which to be thankful. Much more than the man who appeared to be a legless beggar. So he stood up and walked out of the chapel. As he passed by the presbytery, the priest told his counterpart that he was leaving.

"Why are you going?"

The priest answered, "My problem is solved. Everything is all right!"

"Please wait. I will be with you shortly."

"There's no need for that because I found my way out of the crisis. Thank you very much."

And he left.

You see, the reality is that as a human being, you're blessed. But if you're ungrateful, you might think you're unlucky or the world is against you. Guess what? If you think like that, you'll attract bad luck and opposition. On the other hand, if you start to be grateful for the small things and the things you take for granted, you'll begin attracting the big things you want. I know you have more to win by being grateful than by thinking negatively.

For bonuses go to ...

What Do You See?

When you look deep into yourself, what do you see? Do you see a winner or a loser? Do you see life or a dead end? Do you see hope or misery? Do you see a blessing or a waste? The fact is that because you have a brain to think, a mouth to talk, and lungs to breathe, you already represent a powerhouse. You were born to win—to be a victor—and enjoy life.

I believe your job is to start seeing the intangible aspects of yourself and give thanks for them. You're a human being with full potential. When you detect and acknowledge the possibility and blessings within you, your life will change completely.

Whatever you see the most, you'll continue to receive the most. However, if you don't like what you're receiving the most, it's probably time for you to look deeper and start giving thanks for the good you can find within and about yourself.

I read that a man was mad at himself, cursing God because he didn't have shoes, until he saw another man without feet to wear them. Isn't it entirely possible that what you take for granted could be a blessing for someone else?

No matter what you face today, I believe there are many things for which you can be grateful. The simple fact that you can breathe in and out means you already have more than a million reasons to be thankful. There's no doubt that life can be extremely hard, but if you can focus on any positive part you can see, I believe you'll have a happier life. So, see the best in yourself, and be grateful!

> *"Do not be anxious about anything,*
> *but in every situation, by prayer and petition,*
> *with thanksgiving, present your requests to God."*
> **(Philippians 4:6)**

Take Stock of What You Have

Sometimes, it might be hard to be thankful while dealing with a problem. But it would help if you remembered that you're not the only one with challenges. Also, the more you think about a problem, the more problems will come your way. Finally, avoid being anxious because it leads to anxiety, which raises your stress level and stops your body from functioning normally. Anxiety also increases your fear, and fear is a destroyer. Learning to keep anxiety offshore and cope with difficulties through joy is one of the best gifts you can give yourself.

How do you do that?

I've learned a formula from many great leaders and successful business moguls like Oprah Winfrey, Steve Harvey, Les Brown, and Bob Proctor. It's a simple but powerful idea, "Be grateful for what you have." If you're happy and grateful for what you already have, you'll attract more of what you want. And that's what I did when I was homeless for six months in 2013. My attitude of gratefulness kept me from being anxious and led me to a place where I've gotten almost everything I dreamed of.

So, I ask, what's good about you? What do you appreciate in your life? As I said, we tend to take the most precious gifts in our life for granted while chasing material things. Bob Proctor, author of the book *You Were Born Rich*, suggests regularly completing the sentence, "I am happy and grateful that...." Are you alive? Are you healthy? Can you walk, talk, and smell the beauty of life? Can you see? Are you working? Do you have a place to sleep? Do you have a family, bank account, and car to drive? So many things and people for which to be grateful!

One way you can count your blessings is by putting them on paper. Doing this each day upon waking is powerful. You can jot down anything you appreciate about your life, family, workplace, or whatever else makes you feel good. You're doing three things here. First, you think about the things you're grateful for. Second, you write them down. Third, you speak them aloud. That reinforces the power within you, increases your faith and hope, and also puts the law of attraction to work for you. Voltaire once said, "Appreciation is a wonderful thing. It makes what is excellent in others belong to us as well."

GRATITUDE UNLEASHES THE POWER WITHIN YOU, WHILE HOPE PUTS THAT POWER TO WORK TO ACCOMPLISH YOUR DREAMS OR LIFE'S DESIRE.

Change Your Focus

Life is constantly moving; if you're not focusing on going forward, you're going backward. And whether the circumstances of your life get better or worse depends on where you focus. The good news is that you're in control of leading your focus. Someone can give you advice, but you're the only one who can challenge how you focus.

While there are probably many techniques you can use to help change your focus, gratitude is one of the most empowering forces at your disposal. When you're grateful for what you already have, you can't focus on what you don't have. So turn your mind to all the positive parts and circumstances of your life and be grateful for them. Make it a habit to wake up every day and thank God for creating the universe.

And take time to enjoy every little bit of that universe—the trees, flowers, birds, sunshine, sunset, moon, stars, animals, ocean, rivers, and even the air you need to live and stay healthy.

Finally, find reasons to thank your partner, kids, co-workers, managers, and so on.

"Cultivate the habit of being grateful
for every good thing that comes to you,
and give thanks continuously. And because all things
have contributed to your advancement,
you should include all things in your gratitude."
– Ralph Waldo Emerson

Gratitude makes you stronger and helps you open the heart of the universe. Also, when you focus on gratitude, you'll transform your suffering into joy and hope. However, if you think it's too difficult to find the best in everything, simply pause and say, "Thank you, God." That works, too.

For bonuses go to www.BelieveYourHope.com

Notes

Chapter 9

Discipline, the Ugly Duckling of Success

9

*"Discipline is the bridge
between goals and accomplishment."*
— Jim Rohn

The Secret to Success Hides in Plain Sight

Have you ever discovered something important or that you've needed for a long time only to find it was in front of you the entire time? That something is the secret to success.

Allow me to elaborate. I'm talking about the ugly duckling that becomes the swan. I'm talking about the tiny ant that lifts 100 times its weight. I'm talking about the tortoise that raced the hare and won. I'm talking about the powerful engine hidden beneath the hood of a plain-Jane car. I'm talking about the secret that hides in plain sight, masquerades as something else, and seems unknowable and untouchable. It's a powerful secret that consists of many stories in one. And that secret, the secret to success, is discipline.

Discipline is studying, learning, training, and applying a system of standards. When you think of discipline as a choice or decision, you take control—before anyone or anything else. More discipline equals more choice and control, while less discipline results in less choice and control.

However, most people don't see discipline as the secret to success because, at first glance, it can appear ugly. Discipline isn't sexy, doesn't look or feel wonderful, and seems difficult and tedious, but it's easy when you have the will—and the result is beautiful. It gives you the power to achieve what you hope for.

You Can Achieve Anything

Believe it or not, you're a powerful human who can achieve whatever you want. You have the power within you, and it's up to you to use it. But to do so, you must have discipline. Furthermore, no one but you is responsible for your discipline, nor can anyone else use the power within you. You have to believe in it and yourself.

Nothing can stop you if you know where you're going and support that plan with disciplined action. But let me ask:

What are you willing to sacrifice to follow your plan?

Are you disciplined enough to make those sacrifices?

What do you think is stopping you from getting what you want?

Knowing that discipline can lead you to success, would you at least try to overcome those challenges?

And finally, what does discipline mean to you?

Take Responsibility

Shortly after my time as a homeless person in 2013, my good friend Yanm Morales told me he needed his truck back. I worked for a Hyundai dealership then, so I applied for a Hyundai Accent, the cheapest car on the lot. You probably guessed that the banks declined me because my credit was terrible. I then went to the used car manager and asked him to help me because I was living far away from the dealership and desperately needed transportation. He helped me get an old Saturn Ion for $2,995 using in-house financing.

One of the best things that could ever have happened to me was that the "in-house finance bank" also reported to the credit bureau. Knowing this, I decided on disciplined payments. Consequently, I qualified to lease a new Toyota Camry within a year. That was when I knew I controlled my financial destiny and that all I needed was to be responsible and disciplined in everything I did.

> *"Small disciplines repeated with consistency every day lead to great achievements gained slowly over time."*
> *– John C. Maxwell*

If you want to walk from point A to point Z, you must start with the first step and go step-by-step afterward. The same holds for everything you want to integrate into your life. However, I recommend that you be kind to yourself and start by applying discipline to the little tasks you do daily. When you make discipline your habit in small things, it becomes easier to convince yourself to apply discipline to the big stuff.

For example, you can start by getting in the habit of cleaning up clutter at your house. Make it simple. When you wake up in the morning, fix your bed as nicely as possible. I read a book in which the author declared, "If your bedroom is a mess, it's because your brain is a mess." My idea is to be proactive: Start your practice of discipline in your bedroom, and it will transfer to your brain and then to every other thing you want to accomplish.

Be conscious. Know what you do, when you do it, and why you do it. Be disciplined in your job, go to work on time, and dress accordingly. Obey the rules in your house, on the streets, in school, at work, and, more importantly, obey those self-imposed. Be disciplined in your respect for yourself and those around you. And finally, do what you say you will do whether someone is watching or not.

> *"For a man to conquer himself*
> *is the first and noblest of all victories."*
> **– Plato**

The Greatest Gift

Finding yourself is one of the best gifts you can give to humanity (yourself included). Asking questions about yourself begins the process of self-discovery and lends meaning to your life.

- Who are you?
- Where do you come from?
- Why are you here?
- Where are you going?
- What is your purpose in life?

Unless you can find answers to such questions, there's no reason to be disciplined—because your life will have no meaning. So, why don't you cultivate the habit of taking a few minutes each day to be by yourself and work on answering those questions? *The Bible* says, "When you know the truth, the truth will set you free." And the only way you can know the truth is by asking questions. I deeply believe that cultivating the simple practice of asking yourself questions like those listed above will one day bring you answers as clear as the water you drink.

Please be disciplined enough that when the answers pop into your mind, you'll write them down in a notebook. If you don't record the answers, you'll lose them, and I don't believe you want that to happen. Those answers will help you understand who you are, why you're here, and your purpose in life. When you know those things and mix them with discipline, nothing in the world will stop you from achieving your will. **Actualize your hope with discipline plus the right actions.**

"A man is the sum of his actions, of what he has done, of what he can do. Nothing else."
– Gandhi

For bonuses go to ...

Congratulations! It's good that you believe in yourself, have definite goals, and own a set of plans to accomplish them. It's also fantastic that you know who you are and your purpose in life. These things can guide you to do what you want or go where you want. But remember that you must take definite and consistent action to accomplish anything serious. As the saying goes, "You know a man by his actions."

What kind of actions have you taken? What actions are you taking now? What kind of actions would you like to take? It all depends on what you want to achieve and where you want to go. Yet, focus on what you're hopeful for, take the right action every day, blend your focus and actions with discipline, and the world will be yours to conquer.

It's written in *The Bible* that God didn't give us the spirit of fear but power, love, and a sound mind. So fear not, and take action! Look, I don't say you can't fail. But even if you fail, you can start over, and you'll reach your destination in the end— which is nothing less than the realization of your hopes. And while it might look like you're failing, I want to assure you that discipline plus the right actions can't fail.

> ***"No discipline seems pleasant at the time, but painful.***
> ***Later on, however, it produces a harvest***
> ***of righteousness and peace for those***
> ***who have been trained by it."***
> **(Hebrews 12:11)**

I was looking at a video posted on March 18th, 2013, on Bally Sports Cincinnati Twitter.

A journalist asked Lebron James, one of the greatest basketball players of all time, about his training regimen.

"Can you count on one hand the times when you said to yourself, 'I believe I don't feel like doing it today?'"

Lebron answered, "Oh yeah, yeah, yeah. I've had a lot of those times, and then two or three minutes later, I was like, get your ass up. Let's get to work. That's just how I am. We all feel that way. We just, like, we ain't got it today. But, as soon as I feel that, I always think it's somebody else that said, 'Well, I ain't got it today' because he may not be getting none. I don't like that feeling."

The point I want to make is that discipline isn't easy. It takes dedication, strength, and much internal work. In fact, I believe that it requires more work from within than from without. There's always a battle going on in the mind regarding whether to do the right thing or the contrary. Even Lebron James, a superstar in basketball, has confirmed that he always has to deal with that battle. However, he created a mantra to get himself back on track. And I believe it's because of his discipline that he has reached the level of play he has today. On June 2nd, 2022, Forbes Magazine published that the 18-time all-star, four time-time NBA champion, and two-time Olympic gold medalist, Lebron James, officially became the first active NBA player billionaire. He didn't achieve his success on and off the basketball court by luck but rather by exercising tough discipline and a great work ethic.

For bonuses go to ...

**"Whoever heeds discipline shows the way to life,
but whoever ignores correction leads others astray."
(Proverb 10: 17)**

To finish, I would say that if discipline is the engine of success, it makes the world roll in alignment. Discipline creates a peaceful living environment. Discipline helps you raise your children and become a great dad or mom. Discipline creates a safe workplace. Discipline leads you to outstanding achievements. And last but not least, I believe that discipline is what keeps your hope alive. Therefore, I encourage you to be disciplined in every path of life because the fruit of discipline is always sweet.

www.BelieveYourHope.com

Notes

For bonuses go to www.BelieveYourHope.com

Notes

Chapter 10

Hope, Prayer, and Faith

10

*"Be joyful in hope, patient in affliction,
and faithful in prayer."*
(Romans 12:12)

So far, you've read about different techniques to help you achieve your goals and dreams. However, along the way to your achievements, you'll have to deal with difficulties, tough times, and opposition. I believe this is where many people fail, either by halting the pursuit of their heart's desire or not knowing what action(s) to take. Hope, prayer, and faith can make all the difference when you allow them to enter your life.

*"Hope is being able to see that
there is light despite all the darkness."*
– Desmond Tutu

For bonuses go to ...

Hope

It doesn't matter whether you win or lose in life; darkness will sometimes descend upon you, and you can lose hope if you're not strong enough. I've said from the beginning of this book that "hope is infinite." You may first see it as a glimmer in the darkness (for it's the beginning of all great achievements), but hope is always there and is without end. Once you've discovered it, never allow yourself to lose sight of it because when you have hope, you'll never reach the dead end of life.

Nelson Mandela said, "May your choices reflect your hopes, not your fears." It's okay to be fearful. After all, it's an integral part of your survival instinct that warns you of impending danger. But if you freeze instead of taking action, fear can be a powerful destructor of dreams and life. That's where cultivating hope comes into play; it will give you the power to move forward through your fear. So be optimistic in everything you do. Allow your choices to reflect your hope rather than your fear. And I know you'll find your way through your troubles.

Former president of the United States, Barack Obama, said, "Hope is that thing inside us that insists, despite all the evidence to the contrary, that something better awaits us if we have the courage to work for it and to fight for it." So feed your brain with hopeful ideas and dreams. It's a powerful machine always at work; think of one idea, and your brain will always bring you a chain of compatible ideas.

No matter the situation you're dealing with, you can choose to think and act positively rather than negatively. Be proactive rather than reactive! When things aren't working perfectly for you, when you think you're in the darkest day of your life, when you feel that everything is working against you, it's crucial to push yourself to keep fear at bay and focus intensely on your hope.

I would also like you to understand that darkness doesn't actually exist; it's simply the absence of light and isn't to be feared. Moreover, if the sun shone all day and night, you wouldn't be able to enjoy the beauty, brightness, and softness of the moon and stars. So when facing darkness (hardship), look for a different light source. For example, you can think about, imagine, and enjoy reaching your destination. Let that realization of your hope become a light to guide you, just as the moon and stars have guided travellers since the beginning of time.

Finally, it's essential to recognize that fear reflects death, hope reflects infinite life, and you have the power to choose between them.

Prayer

A prayer is an act of communication between you and God. You can choose to pray silently or out loud. You can pray anywhere, anytime, and for any reason. And you don't need to be in trouble before you start praying. He will always listen, and He promises to answer. Because of this, you're never alone. What's more, you have a superpower on your side—one who can move mountains. Be wise enough to ease every kind of pressure you face with prayer.

Your prayer can be a simple thanksgiving, a confession, or a request to your God, but when you pray, do it as if your life depends on it—because it does. Have you ever seen a baby about to fall, and the mother who is far away cries, "Oh my God!" then, in the blink of an eye, is at the baby's feet? Her short prayer to God ensured that nothing could stop her.

Your prayer doesn't have to be long, and there's no need to complicate your communication with God by multiplying your words. *The Bible* says, "But when ye pray, use not vain repetitions, as the heathens do." Keep it simple. Just pray with sincerity and confidence. You can even pray with nothing but hope in mind by saying, "Please, help me, God."

Because he knows what you're going through and is always ready to help. All you have to do is to ask. I would also encourage you to believe in yourself and God and that he will answer your request positively.

Finally, if you're happy and your petitions have been answered, thank God or sing as a sign of gratitude.

What Can Prayer Do?

Prayer keeps you humble but gives you a feeling of security, which comes from knowing that you're not alone, whatever happens. God is always there for you.

Don't keep throwing yourself at a mountain; it's too much to take on alone. And don't carry the heavy load of relationships, financial trouble, or the many other stresses in your life. Instead,

I would insist that you pray and ask God for help. Allow Him to carry some of the load. Also, while you pray, I want you to understand that whatever the circumstances you're enduring, many other people have been there before you, and they survived.

I've been through many situations, including being homeless for six months, and prayer is one of the main things that has kept my joy intact despite all adversities. I would say with all sincerity that no matter what situation you find yourself in, always pray before you do anything else. Ask God for guidance, and let Him help!

*"We are to pray in times of adversity,
lest we become faithless and unbelieving.
We are to pray in times of prosperity,
lest we become boastful and proud.
We are to pray in times of danger,
lest we become fearful and doubting.
We are to pray in times of security,
lest we become self-sufficient."*
– Billy Graham

Faith

You were born with faith. When you were a baby, you had faith in your mom and dad because they were always there and cared for and provided for you. You also had faith in relatives and things in your surroundings. And as you grew, you had faith in yourself, your power to get things done, and your cultures, religion, and God.

> ***"Now faith is the substance of things hoped for, the evidence of things not seen."***
> **– The Bible**

Fear vs Faith

Sometimes your fear may appear to be bigger than your faith. I don't remember who said that fear is "False Evidence Appearing Real," but I strongly agree. Fear is nothing more than your faith that something bad will happen to you or someone else you know. Fear doesn't exist. What you call fear is just faith in the opposite direction. Faith is always there, and Job reminds us of this in the following Bible verse: "For the thing which I greatly feared is come upon me, and which I was afraid of is come upon me."

While someone like me can help you to be conscious of your faith, it's up to you to activate that faith and use it for your good. *The Bible* says, "You can get anything—anything you ask for in prayer—if you have faith."

What is Faith in the Real World?

- Faith is the farmer, who spends his money to prepare the soil and sow the seeds, then maintains high expectations that rain will fall and the seeds will crack open, germinate, grow, and produce.
- Faith is the inventor, Henry Ford, who needed to build a V8 engine without knowing how to do it. However, his faith and passion were so great that time and money were no match, and he did it.
- Faith is Gandhi, who believed he could free his country and people passively—with no violence and never touching a weapon—and did it.
- Faith is when you go to sleep with a strong belief that you'll wake up the next day.
- Faith is the market that opens its door daily with enormous certitude that the customers will come.
- Faith is believing you can achieve your goal and working on it till you get it done—no matter what comes your way.
- Faith is seeing and enjoying your heart's desire in your mind before you ever achieve it.

It's written in *The Bible* that "Whatsoever things ye desire, when ye pray, believe that ye receive them, and ye shall have them?" If you can see it with your mind's eye and enjoy it with your imagination, nothing in the world can stop you from getting what you want—because it's already yours by faith. But beware ... to enjoy the fruit of your faith ... you must be consistent.

For bonuses go to ...

Your Faith is Constantly Under Attack

The world bombards us with opinions and distractions, and it's your responsibility to safeguard the door of your most powerful asset—your faith. The internet overflows with social media like TikTok, Facebook, WhatsApp, Instagram, and Twitter. Their users can share and promote their ideas regarding almost every aspect of life. On the other hand, religions multiply daily, and they all want you to act and believe according to their beliefs. Moreover, your family members, friends, classmates, and co-workers love you so much that they want to guide you toward what they think is best for you.

After listening to these different kinds of information, ideas, and opinions, it's easy to become confused and doubt your faith if you aren't strong enough mentally. Therefore, I believe it's up to you to repel the opinions of people on social media and in sects or religious groups and stick to what you strongly believe in.

How to Strengthen Your Faith

Your faith can save you, and it can destroy you. You can allow it to lift you, or you can stay in misery for the rest of your life. Your faith is the most extraordinary intangible power at your disposal, but it's up to you whether it will be an asset or a liability. Consequently, learning how to strengthen your faith is necessary for your growth.

In his book *Think and Grow Rich*, Napoleon Hill said, "Repetition of affirmation of orders to your subconscious mind is the only known method of voluntary development of the emotion of faith." Are you willing to do the right things to improve your faith? What do you listen to every day, and can you define or classify it? What do you say to yourself when things aren't leaning in your favor? If you take some time to answer these questions, you'll be able to set boundaries regarding what you'll entertain from others, but especially yourself.

Maintaining your faith straight is an unceasing business. It's crucial to clean the filter of your brain every day so that you don't clog it up with opposing ideas and opinions. The noise out there is so loud that if you don't pay attention, you might see your faith derailed before you know it. Therefore, I'm convinced that having a laser focus on your faith is mandatory.

Finally, if you want your faith to bring forth fruit, you need to feed your brain and subconscious mind with positive thoughts repeatedly. Moreover, you must start talking and acting as if you already possess what you want. Because, by your faith, whatever you can imagine with active emotion is already yours.

The Triumvirate

You become unstoppable when you mix your hope with sincere prayer and faith.

Hope gives you a reason to live and keep moving toward your dreams.

For bonuses go to ...

Prayer gives you power and stability because God is always with you and never fails.

Faith ensures that no matter what comes your way, you'll be a winner, not a loser; a victor, not a victim; a go-getter, not a quitter.

Nothing is permanent on this earth; everything comes, and everything goes. So it doesn't make sense to worry or be afraid of loss. Change is the natural cycle of things. Nothing last forever. If one day you find that you're missing someone or something, remember to renew your hope and back that up with prayer and faith.

Ecclesiastes says, "To everything there is a season, and a time to every purpose under the heaven: A time to be born, and a time to die; a time to plant, and a time to pluck up that which is planted; a time to weep, and a time to laugh; a time to mourn, and a time to dance; a time to get, and a time to lose; a time to keep, and a time to cast away."

Therefore, I say unto you that each season or stage in life is just for a moment, and everything will pass. Take the time to understand this. I also encourage you to keep your hope before you, no matter how dark life may seem. Because if you have hope and know that God is your helper, you'll pray. And if you pray with high expectations and strong faith, you give yourself a reason to live.

Live life fully, and live it with hope!

www.BelieveYourHope.com

Notes

For bonuses go to www.BelieveYourHope.com

Notes

Conclusion

When we overcame homelessness, my wife told me she didn't hold onto the idea of suicide because she saw that I kept my composure amid the crisis by always being positive and facing the world with a big smile. That was indeed true, but only because I had hope. So, please remember what I've shared with you in this book . . .

1. Hope is within you.

2. Everything starts from within, but to be successful, you must believe in yourself and your God-given power.

3. *The Bible* says you're a co-creator and a ruler. To act as such requires that you set your intention and have faith that what you intend to pursue is achievable. But what is your intention? It's up to you to select whatever you want from the universe, and as the saying goes, the universe will always say yes to you.

4. Once you determine what you want, you need to set goals and build a plan to reach your destination.

For bonuses go to ...

5. While you work toward your dreams, you must clearly understand what you hope for and visualize it as already being yours.

6. It's necessary to change your vocabulary and the way you talk about yourself and others. Use your words cautiously and intentionally because words have power. If you say you can, then you will; if you say you can't, then you won't. Moreover, don't listen to those who would lead you away from hope and your heart's desire.

7. Be disciplined in every part of your life. The Dalai Lama once said, "A disciplined mind leads to happiness, and an undisciplined mind leads to suffering." I know it isn't easy to be disciplined in everything, but trust me when I say suffering is much harder. I encourage you to practice self-discipline.

8. Be grateful for everything good in your life—great and small. Be thankful for what you have and for what you expect to get. No matter how you live today, there's someone somewhere who would prefer to be like you, so be joyful, give thanks to God, and focus on what you hope will come.

9. Keep in mind that everything that comes will someday pass. Whether it's your family members, friends, money, material possessions, health, or career, I assure you that nothing is there forever. So find joy in it all—every day. Follow the wise

counsel in *The Bible*: "This is the day that the Lord has made; let us rejoice and be glad in it."

10. When you know there's joy to be found in every day, and believe it, not even death can shake you. Even if you lose everything you hold dear, you have three untouchable things you can rely upon. And no matter how deep you fall or how dark your life seems, you can be sure of eventual victory. These three foundational tools can lend you patience, persistence, perseverance, and strength. What are they? **Hope, sincere prayer to God, and faith**.

As I said previously, good and bad things will happen to you. But if you maintain a laser focus on your hope, pray often, have faith that God will hear those prayers, and do all you can to enjoy a beautiful life, you'll prevail. Because I strongly believe that **Hope is nothing less than God within you.**

So allow me to finish with a form of blessing taken from *The Bible*:

"May the Lord bless and protect you; may the Lord's face radiate with joy because of you; may he be gracious to you, show you his favor, and give you his peace."

Amen!

About the Author

Born and raised in Haiti, Alex Dorcius came to live with his nuclear family in Miami, Florida, in 1997.

He attended Miami Dade College (MDC), earning an Associate Degree in Arts; Florida International University (FIU), graduating with a Bachelor's Degree in Communication Arts; and Ashworth College, where he obtained a Diploma with Honors in Personal Financial Planning.

Alex is a professional sales consultant who has been in that field for over a decade. He considers himself a hopeful man and does everything with the intent to excel. Through many years of network marketing, Alex maintained a position in leadership groups, which pushed him to read hundreds of books on leadership and personal development. Networking success is determined by how many people you help to be successful, and it taught him to love people. Alex keeps that heritage with him: to love and care enough to help others.

There's no doubt that Alex has experienced many failures. But the man has also had many successes and says he learned the critical importance of enjoying and celebrating them. Even more crucial, however, is motivating yourself to push through failures by focusing on hope. Because of these things, Alex also works as a motivational coach who teaches people how to focus on their hope, achieve their dreams, and live happy lives. He says, "No matter how bad things look (or are), I always see the best in people near me. I can't emphasize enough that I love each and every human being and strive to help those around me keep their hope alive and better themselves."

Alex believes in God, and that He is always with us. He is the One who gives us hope. And if there is hope, there is life. As it says in *The Bible*, "Everything is possible."

Alex is married and lives in the Sunshine State of Florida.

Made in the USA
Columbia, SC
03 October 2024